Cuba Confronts the
World Crisis of the '90s
CHE GUEVARA AND THE FIGHT FOR SOCIALISM TODAY

by Mary Alice Waters

PATHFINDER
NEW YORK   LONDON   MONTREAL   SYDNEY

Copyright © 1992 by Pathfinder Press
All rights reserved

ISBN 978-0-87348-760-3
Library of Congress Control Number 93217038

Manufactured in Canada

First edition, 1992
Thirteenth printing, 2025

COVER DESIGN: Toni Gorton

COVER PHOTO: Agricultural brigade in Havana Province
(Marice Cohn Band/*Miami Herald*)

PATHFINDER
pathfinderpress.com
Email: pathfinder@pathfinderpress.com

CONTENTS

Introduction
Argiris Malapanis   5

**CHE GUEVARA AND
THE FIGHT FOR SOCIALISM TODAY**
Mary-Alice Waters   13

Notes   47

Introduction

BY ARGIRIS MALAPANIS

"DO YOU HAVE ANY BOOKS by this Cuban guy, Che?" José, a worker at the Smithfield meat-packing plant in Landover, Maryland, asked me last September. He was driving his car out of the factory gate when he stopped to talk with a group of young people distributing campaign literature for James Warren and Estelle DeBates, Socialist Workers Party candidates for U.S. president and vice-president in the 1992 elections. José said he was interested in socialism and, although he hadn't yet read anything by Che, knew he was "one of the best socialists to ever come around."

The next day a team of young supporters of Warren and DeBates was campaigning at the University of Maryland. We found the same kind of interest among many students in books about the Cuban revolution, including those by and about Ernesto Che Guevara.

"Who was Che?" asked Robert, a student helping out at the campaign table for the first time. He had just taken part in several long discussions on Cuba with other students from Lebanon and Ethiopia. "Is it true there isn't a dictatorship in Cuba? Why did the Stalinist regimes shatter in the Soviet Union and Eastern Europe? Won't the same thing happen in Cuba as in Russia?"

This pamphlet discusses the ideas of Che Guevara on

how to organize workers and farmers to make the transition to socialism—and how to make sure that "the same thing" doesn't happen in Cuba, and all the future Cubas, as happened in Russia.

For Che, this was not a matter of arm-chair speculation. Che was an Argentine-born revolutionary who joined the struggle to overthrow the Batista dictatorship in Cuba in the mid-1950s and became one of the central leaders of the revolutionary government that triumphed in the Caribbean island in January 1959. He was killed by U.S.-trained troops in Bolivia in October 1967 while leading a guerrilla struggle whose goal was to overthrow the tyrannical regime there.

This pamphlet explains the current relevance of the perspectives Che lived and fought for to the challenges confronting the Cuban revolution in the world of the 1990s. These perspectives are important not only for the Cuban people—who are struggling through tremendous economic difficulties today—but for youth and working people the world over.

Will Cuba survive the economic problems it faces? Is socialism the cause of these difficulties? What about the thirty-plus-year U.S. trade embargo against Cuba? Is it still possible to fight for socialism today?

These and other questions discussed in this pamphlet by Mary-Alice Waters are ones I've been posed with time and again, not only as I've campaigned for the socialist alternative in the 1992 U.S. elections, but also as I've traveled to many countries over the last two years as a representative of the Young Socialist Alliance attending meetings sponsored by the World Federation of Democratic Youth (WFDY) and other organizations. I've found young people who've insisted on discussing these questions in Jerusalem and other towns in the West Bank and the Gaza Strip; in Nicosia, Cyprus; Athens, Greece; Belgrade, Dubrovnik, and Sarajevo in the former Yugoslavia; and Mexico City, São Paulo, and other cities in Latin America.

The contents of this pamphlet first appeared as the introduction to the 1992 French-language edition, published by Pathfinder, of *Che Guevara: Economics and Politics in the Transition to Socialism* by Cuban economist Carlos Tablada. This is the companion volume to Pathfinder's English-language edition published in 1990; the Spanish-language edition was issued in Cuba in 1987. Pathfinder also publishes several works by Che Guevara, including *Socialism and Man in Cuba*—in English, Spanish, French, and several other languages; *Che Guevara Speaks*, first published in 1967, within weeks of Guevara's murder; and *Che Guevara and the Cuban Revolution*, the most comprehensive single-volume collection of his writings and speeches.

The author of this booklet, Mary-Alice Waters, is the editor of the Marxist magazine *New International* and of the recent Pathfinder book, *To Speak the Truth: Why Washington's 'Cold War' against Cuba Doesn't End*, a collection of four speeches by Fidel Castro and Che Guevara presented over a span of two decades before the United Nations.

◆

Hundreds of thousands of workers, peasants, students, and others poured into the streets of São Paulo and other cities in Brazil in the fall of 1992 demanding the ouster of the country's corrupt president, Fernando Collor de Mello. University students led many of the marches, which were a factor in Collor's fall.

Should young people look to some other section of Brazil's "national bourgeoisie" for a way out of the economic and social catastrophe facing working people there? Can working people, by joining in the unfolding struggles, forge a revolutionary party that can lead them in taking power out of the hands of the capitalist class and establishing a workers' and peasants' government? Even if so, how can they then begin to build a society that will put human needs before profits that enrich only a tiny handful of already wealthy families? What can workers learn from the Cuban revolution? Why did Che so strongly oppose the economic policies of the Stalinist regimes in Eastern Europe and the former Soviet Union?

These questions are being hotly debated at meetings, marches, and rallies not just in Brazil but throughout Latin America, which remains mired in an economic depression. The viewpoint explained in this pamphlet—based on the experience of thirty-three years of the Cuban revolution—is becoming more relevant than ever as working people resist the devastation of their livelihoods wrought by capitalism. More than seven hundred marches have taken place this year against the Venezuelan government's austerity measures, for example. Strikes and demonstrations erupted in Ecuador in September 1992 after the government devalued the currency by nearly 30 percent, causing prices of many basic goods to double.

Many topics Waters deals with here were those I heard discussed over and over during a June 1992 conference of political parties from the Americas held in Argentina. The meeting marked the sixty-fourth anniversary of Guevara's birth and was held in his native city, Rosario. Just after the conference, thousands of students demonstrated against government education cutbacks in the streets of Buenos Aires, Argentina's capital. Both in Rosario and at the student protests, dozens of young people and others bought copies of Pathfinder books with speeches by Guevara. Interest was particularly high in the exchange of views on "Che Guevara, Cuba, and the Road to Socialism" in issue no. 8 of the Marxist magazine *New International*.

At a congress of the Communist youth of Colombia in Bogotá a few months later, participants purchased every copy we had brought with us of the Spanish-language edition of *New International* no. 8 off a Pathfinder literature table, as well as all the copies of *Socialism and Man in Cuba* by Che (and several more were ordered by mail). Afterwards, representatives of youth organizations from throughout the Americas affiliated with the World Federation of Democratic Youth met in Bogotá and decided to organize a continent-wide youth brigade to Cuba at the end of 1992. Brigadistas will work alongside Cuban volunteers as part of the effort by the Cuban people to achieve food self-sufficiency.

As discussed by Waters, this accelerated food program, involving hundreds of thousands of Cubans in voluntary work brigades, was launched by the government of Cuba in 1990 when trade with its former major trading partners—the Soviet Union and Eastern European countries—began to collapse. The youth leaders in Bogotá gave the internationalist brigade a fitting name: the Ernesto Che Guevara Youth of the Americas Brigade in Solidarity with Cuba.

Guevara was the foremost proponent of voluntary work as a way working people can fight to cease being the objects of blind economic laws and begin instead to collectively shape their own living and working conditions and social relations, and change themselves in the process. Waters describes how the revival of the voluntary work movement in Cuba in the mid-1980s was instrumental in beginning to reverse the political retreat going back a decade earlier when policies of planning and management copied from the Soviet Union were generalized throughout Cuba.

Further evidence of the interest in the challenges facing revolutionary Cuba today is the turnout for a fall 1992 U.S. speaking tour by Cuban youth leaders Ibis Alvisa González and José Antonio Concepción Rángel. More than three thousand students and other young people attended campus and community meetings in ten U.S. cities. What's more, on October 1, for the first time in more than thirty years, an advertised public meeting for Cuban revolutionaries was held on a Miami, Florida, campus, where more than two hundred students and others hotly debated the same questions addressed in this booklet. It was a pleasure taking part in that meeting and offering books by Che Guevara for sale in English, Spanish, and French.

But it's not only in the Americas that I've discovered the attraction of—and the controversy around—Che Guevara and the Cuban revolution. Interest was also high among the more than one thousand students and workers at a summer 1992 conference of youth from the Balkans and other European countries called to protest military intervention in the former Yugoslavia by the U.S., German, and other imperialist governments. Following the conference, held in northern Greece at the border with Yugoslavia, I traveled to Belgrade, where knowledge of the Cuban revolution is minimal compared to neighboring capitalist countries. Nonetheless, several students at the University of Belgrade wanted to find out how Che's ideas were relevant to their fight to end the carnage in that country and to begin its genuine transformation into a truly human society.

The reach of Che's words, and the example of his deeds, extends to Asia, too. The Socialist Youth of Japan, for example, has undertaken to translate a number of Guevara's works into Japanese from the English-language Pathfinder editions. During a U.S. speaking tour this year, Peter Mokaba, president of the African National Congress (ANC) Youth League, hailed revolutionary Cuba's consistent support for the South African freedom struggle. A victorious revolution in South Africa, Mokaba said, would mean, in a qualitative new way, that "Cuba is not alone"—the goal for which Che Guevara, too, was fighting when he was brutally murdered in Bolivia a quarter century ago.

OCTOBER 8, 1992

Che Guevara and the fight for socialism today

BY MARY-ALICE WATERS

THE OPENING OF THE 1990S is a particularly apt moment for the appearance of this French-language edition of *Che Guevara: Economics and Politics in the Transition to Socialism* by Cuban author Carlos Tablada. World capitalism is mired in a depression marked by staggering debt, instability of the banking system, and mounting social ills such as rising unemployment, homelessness, and a resurgence of epidemic diseases. Bonapartist and ultrarightist currents rear their heads and grow. Economic and social conditions of working people in Africa and much of Latin America and Asia have declined without letup for nearly two decades. Throughout the capitalist world, class inequalities are widening, social polarization and segregation grow, democratic rights are under pressure, cop brutality is on the rise, and rival national ruling classes are intensifying conflicts with each other and pressing toward new and bloodier wars such as the onslaught against the Iraqi people in 1991.

Since late 1989, moreover, the bureaucratized regimes and Communist parties throughout Eastern Europe and then in the former Soviet Union itself have shattered in the face of irresolvable economic, social, and political crises. The methods of planning and management employed, with this or that variation, in each of these countries were for decades promoted as the only road from capitalism to socialism by the big majority of those in the world who called themselves communists.

The alternative—and irreconcilably different—course advanced by Ernesto Che Guevara during the opening years of the Cuban revolution in the early 1960s is the topic of this book.

The verdict on the so-called Soviet model has now been rendered by history: the USSR and Eastern European countries were moving *away from* socialism, not toward it. Well prior to the events of the last several years, revolutionaries in the government and Communist Party of Cuba had begun to seek ways to combat the accelerating corrosive consequences of the methods copied from the Soviet Union, which had been increasingly applied in Cuba since the early 1970s. In 1986 the Communist Party launched what was called the "rectification process," in response to growing evidence of political demobilization and demoralization among working people in Cuba as a result of these policies. One by-product of this "revolution within the revolution," as Fidel Castro referred to it in November 1987,[1] was a renewed interest in learning about the theoretical and practical contributions of Che Guevara to the building of socialism in Cuba.

Having served as a Rebel Army commander in the struggle that toppled the U.S.-backed dictatorship of Fulgencio Batista in January 1959, Guevara shouldered a broad range of duties over the next six years in the new revolutionary government and its political leadership. During this period the Cuban workers and farmers consolidated their political power and expropriated the domestic and foreign landlords and capitalists. The Cuban toilers and their revolutionary leadership began building a communist party capable of organizing working people to defend their revolution, to aid others in the Americas and around the world starting down the same road, and to begin the transition to socialism.

Born in Rosario, Argentina, in 1928, Guevara had been trained as a physician. He traveled throughout Latin America and became involved in anti-imperialist political activity while living in Guatemala in 1954 during the period of the elected government of Jacobo Arbenz. Following the overthrow of that government in a CIA-organized coup, Guevara was forced to leave Guatemala and went to Mexico City. There he met Fidel Castro in mid-1955 and enlisted in the guerrilla expedition Castro was organizing to overthrow the Batista regime. His Cuban compañeros nicknamed him "Che," a popular form of greeting in Argentina.

In late November and early December 1956 Guevara was part of the expedition that sailed to Cuba aboard the yacht *Granma* to begin the revolutionary armed struggle in the Sierra Maestra mountains. Initially the troop doctor, by mid-1957 he was commanding a column of the Rebel Army as well as organizing Marxist education for its cadres. Following the victory in 1959 he served as head of the Department of Industry of the National Institute of Agrarian Reform (INRA); was president of Cuba's National Bank during the crucial year 1960 when domestic- and foreign-owned banks were nationalized, along with most industries; and became head of the Ministry of Industry when it was established in February 1961. Guevara represented Cuba on many trips abroad, in front of the United Nations, and at numerous international conferences.

This book by Carlos Tablada is a study of Guevara's political and theoretical contributions to the economics and politics of the transition to socialism, the product of Che's work as part of the communist leadership of Cuba's working class. "The author," Fidel Castro remarked in an October 1987 speech, "compiled, studied, and presented in a book the essence of Che's economic ideas, retrieved from many of his speeches and writings—articles and speeches dealing with a subject so decisive in the building of socialism."[2] For a French-speaking readership, most of these articles and speeches by Guevara have either not been translated previously or are long out of print.

The enduring political value of Guevara's ideas and example was discussed by Castro at some length at the October 1987 ceremony marking the twentieth anniversary of Guevara's murder at the hands of U.S.-trained troops in Bolivia. Guevara had left Cuba in April 1965 to carry out internationalist missions abroad, with the aim of extending the socialist revolution.

"What I ask for modestly at this twentieth anniversary," Castro said in the 1987 talk, "is that Che's economic thought be made known; that it be known here, in Latin America, in the world: in the developed capitalist world, in the Third World, and in the socialist world." It is with the aim of helping in this task that Pathfinder Press in 1989 published an English translation of Carlos Tablada's book and is now publishing this first French edition. Fidel Castro's October 1987 speech, which provides one of the best possible introductions to the place of Che's contributions as part of the living political continuity of the Cuban revolution, serves as the prologue.

◆

The long emancipation struggle of Cuban working people dates back to the first war of independence against Spanish colonialism, which began in 1868. From the crucible of these and subsequent battles emerged leaders such as Antonio Maceo, Maximo Gómez, and José Martí, whose words and revolutionary deeds left a heritage of anti-imperialist intransigence, internationalism, political integrity, selflessness, and courage. The leadership that left Mexico on the Granma in 1956 drew strength from this rich revolutionary continuity in uncompromisingly leading the transition

CINDY JAQUITH/MILITANT

Volunteer construction workers in Havana, 1990.

from Cuba's national democratic revolution that brought a workers' and farmers' government to power in the fall of 1959 to the socialist revolution that accelerated in late 1960 and early 1961 in response to the hostile actions of domestic and foreign reaction, above all U.S. imperialism.

The socialist road that Cuban working people set out on at the beginning of the 1960s had been opened some four decades earlier by the October 1917 revolution in Russia. The Bolshevik Party leadership headed by V.I. Lenin went through the world's first experiences in organizing workers and peasants to begin the building of socialism in the course of fighting to advance the world revolution. These efforts, from late 1917 through the end of Lenin's active political life in March 1923, left an invaluable legacy to revolutionists such as Guevara and Castro who later sought to continue Lenin's course. The record of the Soviet government, Communist Party, and Communist International in Lenin's time is rich in lessons in the economics and politics of the transition from capitalism to socialism.

The socialist revolution, as Guevara explains repeatedly in the works cited by Tablada, marks the first time in history that expanding political participation and revolutionary consciousness of the toiling majority becomes necessary to the economic organization of society. The door is opened for working people to cease being the objects of blind economic laws that determine their living and working conditions and social relations, and instead to begin placing society's productive forces under their own conscious control.

This is not optional, not just one way among others following a successful popular revolution to advance the transition to socialism. The most committed and self-sacrificing vanguard of the working people, organized in a communist party, *must* lead growing layers of their class in taking more and more control over the political direction and administration of the state and economy. This is the *only* way workers can transform themselves as they collectively transform the social relations under which they work, produce, and live. It is the only way they can make these social relations among human beings more and more open and direct—tearing away the veils and fetishes behind which the capitalist system hides the brutal consequences of its exploitation of toilers and obscures the unique contribution of labor to all social and cultural progress. Along any other road, society will not advance toward socialism and communism, but will instead—mired in bureaucratic planning and management—regress toward capitalism.

"Our revolution nationalized the domestic economy; it nationalized basic industry, including mining," Guevara explained in an August 1961 speech to a conference of Latin American government officials in Punta del Este, Uruguay. "It nationalized all foreign trade, which is now in the hands of the state, and which we proceeded to diversify by trading with the whole world. It nationalized the banking system in order to have in its hands the efficient instrument with which to exercise the function of credit in accordance with the country's needs. It provides for the participation of the workers in the management of the planned national economy."[3]

The fundamentally *political* character of economic questions and decisions during the transition to socialism is central to Guevara's writings and speeches. His contributions in this regard, like those of Lenin, extend well beyond what is normally, and narrowly, thought of as "economics." Che constantly stressed the inseparable interrelationship between the transformation of the social relations of production and the transformation of the political and social consciousness of the working people carrying out this revolutionary process. "To build communism it is necessary, simultaneously with the new material foundations, to build the new man," as he put it in his 1965 article, "Socialism and Man in Cuba."[4]

Thus, Tablada's extensive summary of Guevara's views encompasses a wide range of economic and political questions that confronted revolutionary Cuba. These include:

• the unique character of the transition from capitalism to socialism in contrast to all previous transitions in the history of class society;

• the role of increasing political consciousness and growing control of industry by working people, without which this transition will not only never be achieved, but will slide back toward what Fidel Castro, at the beginning of the rectification process, called "a system worse than capitalism";[5]

• the need for a revolutionary leadership of the working class, a communist party;

• the ways in which market, that is, commodity relations carried over from capitalism (the "law of value"), do or do not continue to operate in aspects of production and distribution during the transition period: in relations between the state, private, and cooperative sectors; between state enterprises and consumers; and between state enterprises themselves and their transactions with vital social institutions such as schools and hospitals;

- how a course can be charted to consciously and progressively restrict the field of operation of the law of value and its reactionary social consequences;
- the changing function of money, banking, and prices;
- the crucial place of a state monopoly over banking, foreign currency reserves and trade, and domestic wholesale trade;
- the obstacles posed by the use of capitalist categories such as "profitability" in judging social costs and benefits, and in guiding a revolutionary government in the organization of production to advance its goals;
- the problem of international commerce at world market prices, which siphons to imperialist owners an exorbitant portion of the value created by the labor of workers and peasants in the Third World, and the internationalist responsibilities of industrially advanced workers' states in the face of this situation;
- the need to transform social attitudes toward work, and the relationship of this goal to the wage structure, forms of incentives, production norms, encouragement to attain higher educational and skill levels, and voluntary work; and
- the political leadership qualities needed by communists engaged in the construction of socialism, whether on production lines and in the fields, in the administration of state enterprises and institutions, or in the apparatus of the government, armed forces, and Communist Party.

In 1963–64 a public discussion touching on many of these questions took place in several Cuban journals. This debate reflected growing conflict between two irreconcilable approaches to economic planning and management, both of which were being used in Cuba during those years. Guevara championed what was called the budgetary finance system, which was being applied under his direction in state enterprises responsible to the Ministry of Industry (some 70 percent of Cuban industry). The other was known as the economic accounting system (or sometimes the financial self-management system). Drawing heavily on contemporary experience in the USSR and Eastern Europe, this system was in use in enterprises organized by the National Institute of Agrarian Reform, then headed by Carlos Rafael Rodríguez, as well as in those accountable to the Ministry of Foreign Trade, directed by Alberto Mora. The articles written by Guevara in the course of this rich discussion are frequently and generously cited by Tablada.[6]

As Guevara worked to help lay a theoretical foundation for the transition to socialism in Cuba, he was in the thick of daily central leadership responsibilities in the revolutionary government and party. Many photographs reproduced in this book record his activity as he carried out this work: his frequent meetings with assemblies of workers in various factories and enterprises and his participation in Sunday voluntary work mobilizations on priority social projects. Guevara immersed himself in the literature discussing the most modern industrial processes in use in other countries. He learned the principles of accounting and took classes in mathematics so he could help advance the application of computerization to economic planning and financial control in Cuba, a task he considered vital.

Guevara also reached back time and again to the lessons drawn by communist leaders from the experiences of previous generations of working people. He had begun this study of Marxism in his late teens, long before meeting Fidel Castro and other leaders of the July 26 Movement from Cuba. He began reading some of the main works of Karl Marx (whom he affectionately referred to in letters as "St. Karl") and Frederick Engels, the founders of the modern communist workers' movement, and of Russian communist leader V.I. Lenin. In 1954, 1955, and 1956 Guevara concentrated on political economy through an extensive study of Marx's *Capital*. Later, as part of his revolutionary work in Cuba, he sought to deepen his knowledge of Lenin's writings and speeches from the opening years of the workers' and peasants' republic in Soviet Russia and from congresses of the Communist International. He frequently went back to *Capital*, *The Critique of the Gotha Programme*, and other works by Marx and Engels, including their rich, pre-Marxist writings from prior to 1847.

References to these works by Marx, Engels, and Lenin occur throughout Guevara's speeches and articles. Speaking before a crowd of several hundred thousand Cubans in October 1967, little more than a week after Che's murder, Castro pointed out how Guevara had ceaselessly worked to deepen his understanding of Marxism and combine that knowledge with concrete experience in order not only to advance the worldwide fight for national liberation and socialism but to help lead Cuban working people in the peaceful construction of socialism:

> If we looked through the windows of his offices, he had the lights on until all hours of the night, studying, or rather, working or studying. For he was a student of all problems; he was a tireless reader.

> His thirst for learning was practically insatiable, and the hours he stole from sleep he devoted to study.[7]

◆

The accomplishments of the workers and farmers of Cuba, many of which are recounted in these pages, including their unstinting internationalism, have earned the views of their communist leadership a hearing in any discussion on the transition from capitalism to socialism. A serious consideration of these matters is otherwise impossible, since the experience of the socialist revolution in Cuba cannot be abstracted from the history of the twentieth century, nor from the future of the twenty-first.

Starting from an oppressive legacy of colonial and semicolonial domination at the time of the revolution in 1959, the Cuban toilers through their labor and political commitment transformed social and economic conditions in that country. This transformation—unprecedented, and thus far unrepeated elsewhere in the colonial world—has strengthened the worker-peasant alliance that formed the bedrock of the revolution and its progress from the outset of the struggle in the Sierra Maestra. These economic and social conquests have been registered despite Washington's unrelenting military pressure and despite its ongoing economic embargo, measures aimed at eroding popular support inside Cuba and around the world for the government's revolutionary course.

- Land to till was provided to poor peasants, sharecroppers, tenant farmers, and other rural working people, along with credit at low interest and access to needed supplies. On a voluntary basis over the subsequent thirty years, roughly half of Cuban peasants, holding some 60 percent of land with private title were organized in farming cooperatives. Most of the former capitalist-owned sugar plantations and many large farms and ranches were organized as state farms, which today encompass some 80 percent of Cuba's agricultural land.

• The production of sugar, Cuba's main export, was in substantial part mechanized, including the backbreaking tasks of harvesting. This modernization made it possible to expand sugar output on state farms and cooperatives while reducing the number of cane cutters from 350,000 before 1959 to one-fifth that number today. This freed up labor for diversified farm production, industrialization, needed construction projects, and social services vital to working people such as education and health care.

• The revolution brought electrification to the big majority of Cuba's rural working people, as well as to the previously poorest layers of the urban working class. Industry, largely restricted to light consumer goods prior to the revolution, has been spread to the production of sugar harvesting combines, automated steelmaking, machine tools, electronic equipment, biotechnology, refrigerators and other household goods, and automatic and semiautomatic weapons. Unlike Third World countries still dominated by imperialism, the benefits from economic modernization in Cuba have been used to improve the living and job conditions of working people, not to enrich a handful of foreign and domestic capitalist families.

• A massive literacy campaign in 1961 mobilized 100,000 young people to go into the countryside to teach Cubans to read and write. As a result, illiteracy was virtually eliminated. Since that time a campaign to bring the vast majority of Cubans up to a sixth-grade education level has been successfully completed, and the population is on its way to achieving a universal ninth-grade level of education. Throughout the rest of Latin America, illiteracy averages nearly 30 percent of the population.

• A system of legal segregation and race discrimination similar to that which existed throughout the Jim Crow South of the United States in 1959 was outlawed with the triumph of the revolution. And the new laws were enforced. As Nelson Mandela, president of the African National Congress, told the Cuban people on July 26, 1991, the revolution's "consistent commitment to the systematic eradication of racism is unparalleled."[8] The results are everywhere evident in Cuba, especially among the generation that has grown up within the revolution, which today comprises the majority of the population.

• A similar commitment to advancing social and economic equality of women has in thirty years brought about changes in women's status that took 150 years or more to accomplish in what are today the most industrialized capitalist countries.

• A concentration of effort and resources on primary health care, training of doctors and other medical personnel, development of a family doctor system, and the construction of hospitals and clinics has reaped impressive gains. Life expectancy and infant mortality rates compare favorably with industrially developed capitalist countries.

• Moreover, Cuban working people have placed their revolutionary government, their resources, and their skills at the service of oppressed and exploited peoples in struggle throughout the Americas, Africa, and Asia. Many hundreds of thousands of Cubans have volunteered to serve as construction workers, engineers, doctors, teachers, technicians, and soldiers—from Nicaragua to Ethiopia, from Vietnam to Mozambique. Some 300,000 Cubans went to Angola as internationalist volunteers between 1975 and 1988 to aid its government and people in defending themselves against South African invaders and imperialist-backed counterrevolutionaries.

The victory at Cuito Cuanavale in southern Angola in the first months of 1988 by the Angolan army, Cuban volunteers, and the South West Africa People's Organisation dealt a decisive military defeat to aggression by Pretoria. The apartheid regime was compelled to sign an agreement that led to Namibia's independence in March 1990 and allowed the return home of the last of Cuba's military volunteers in May 1991. "The defeat of the apartheid army was an inspiration to the struggling people inside South Africa!" said Mandela in his speech to the July 26, 1991, rally in Cuba. "Cuito Cuanavale has been a turning point in the struggle to free the continent and our country from the scourge of apartheid!"[9]

◆

Despite these achievements, the leadership of the Communist Party of Cuba came to the conclusion in the mid-1980s that serious political errors had begun to accumulate during the 1970s and early 1980s that "could have reached the point of being irreversible. We had to rectify them in time," Fidel Castro explained at the December 1986 session of the congress of the Communist Party of Cuba. Doing so, Castro said, involved reaffirming "essential concepts about what socialism is and how it can be built."[10]

Following Che's departure from Cuba in 1965 to carry out internationalist missions, Castro said in the 1987 speech that serves as the prologue to this book, some of his "ideas were incorrectly interpreted and, what's more, incorrectly applied. Certainly no serious attempt was ever made to put them into practice, and there came a time when ideas diametrically opposed to Che's economic thought began to take over."

As a result, while "much has been done to recall his other qualities," Castro said, Che's contribution on these matters "has been largely ignored in our country." The publication of this book by Carlos Tablada in 1987 helped initiate a timely discussion on Guevara's economic thought, in the political context of the rectification process begun the previous year.

Che would have been "appalled" by the road that Cuba had begun to head down, Castro explained in the October 1987 speech, "for he knew that communism could never be attained by wandering down those worn capitalist paths and that to follow along those paths would mean eventually to forget all ideas of solidarity and even internationalism."

Even the Communist Party itself "was starting to go to pot," Castro said in his closing address to the November–December 1986 party congress session. "But we have reacted in plenty of time so that the party members will not be corrupted, the party will not be corrupted, the young people will not be corrupted, and above all our working class will not be corrupted."[11] Rectification went hand in hand with continuing efforts to transform the Communist Party, which encompasses the vanguard of working people in Cuba. Steps toward advancing the proletarian composition of the party's membership and leadership were taken at the February 1986 session of the party congress that immediately preceded and opened the way to the rectification course. In his report on the new Central Committee elected at that congress, Castro stressed the importance of the steps that had been taken to bring into the leadership more factory workers, more Cubans who are Black, more women, more youth, and more veterans of internationalist missions.[12]

Speaking to the Union of Young Communists in April 1987, Castro explained that over the previous fifteen years the course being charted in Cuba had begun to be justified by the concept that various economic and political mechanisms "would automatically solve problems; the idyllic notion, the stupid notion that mechanisms would do the Party's work for it, that they would build socialism, that they would promote development."[13]

The governmental structure of People's Power, for example, "was a great advance, unquestionably," when it was established in the mid-1970s in Cuba, Castro had explained at the November–December 1986 session of the party congress. But "the naive belief came about that following these changes, these steps forward, the state was going to function perfectly, almost automatically. Later we started to realize that this called for very important political work, an immense task for the party."[14]

Other methods cited by Castro that were gaining increased acceptance in Cuba while undermining political consciousness were numerous concepts borrowed either from the USSR or directly from capitalism:

- increasing distribution of food and other necessities through the market at prices determined by supply and de-

mand rather than prioritized to meet social needs;
  • evaluation of economic performance of state enterprises measured by their profitability, rather than by their production of socially necessary goods and services, based on strict cost accounting to minimize the expenditure of human labor, material resources, and limited foreign currency reserves for any given output;
  • growing competition and market/commodity relations among state-owned enterprises and institutions themselves; and
  • increasing reliance on bonuses and individual material incentives while expenditures on the "social wage" (housing, health, education, day care) stagnated, thus widening social inequalities.

"Cuba will never adopt methods, styles, philosophies or characteristics of capitalism," Castro told the quarter million Cubans in Santiago de Cuba who turned out for the annual July 26 rally in 1988. "Socialism and capitalism are two diametrically different things, by definition and by essence."[15]

Even state property and the state monopoly of foreign trade, of control over foreign currency transactions and reserves—vital conquests of the Cuban revolution, and the foundation for maintaining the worker-peasant alliance—could not lead toward socialism unless Cuban working people were mobilized to use these tools consciously and politically to advance that goal. While these revolutionary measures were necessary to break the domination of capitalist social relations and make possible economic planning, they alone were not sufficient to advance the construction of socialism.

"The construction of socialism . . . is fundamentally a

political and revolutionary task," Castro explained, echoing one of Guevara's most important themes reviewed in the pages that follow. "We must help raise people's consciousness. The other mechanisms, the economic factors, are means, or auxiliary tools for political and revolutionary work required by a genuine revolution, and, especially, required for the construction of socialism and the path to communism."[16]

Using the economic priorities and methods borrowed from the USSR as a guide was having corrupting political consequences among a growing social layer in Cuban society. Castro explained at the November–December 1986 session of the party congress that in the years leading up to the launching of the rectification process, a layer of administrators had emerged in state enterprises who "dressed up like capitalists, began to act like capitalists, but without the capitalists' efficiency."[17] They set easily achievable annual production goals in order to garner unearned "overfulfillment" bonuses for themselves and layers of relatively privileged workers. They were obsessed by surpassing quantitative quotas, but couldn't care less about the *quality* of goods for use by the Cuban people. They hoarded and wasted raw materials, and sold shoddy, overpriced goods to other state enterprises, institutions, and consumers. They cooked their ledgers in order to appear "profitable" in money terms, while paying no attention to the true costs to society in terms of squandered resources and labor time. Their own self-seeking, petty-bourgeois example in turn undermined full use of the working day to advance production for the benefit of society, eroded workers' consciousness and discipline, and deepened cynicism.

"Whenever there is a clash between the interests of an

Che Guevara speaking with sugarcane workers, 1963.

enterprise and the interests of the revolution and society," Castro explained in April 1987, "the interests of the revolution and of society must prevail."[18]

"We are not going to have our socialist enterprises competing with each other," he emphasized at the 1986 party congress, "because that has nothing to do with the idea and conception of socialism; it has nothing to do with Marxism-Leninism. They can emulate each other but that's not competition in capitalist fashion, with its dramatic consequences." Instead of factory administrators who operate along these lines, he said, a goal of the rectification process must be that the person in charge of a state enterprise, whether a member of the party or not, "must truly be a communist . . . a revolutionary! And not a communist playing at capitalism, a communist dressed up as a capitalist, or, mark you, a capitalist dressed up as a communist."[19]

This alone would not solve the problems even at the factory level, however. The workers and unions must no longer leave decisions about costs, quality, and performance "to the wise men, the brains, the technocrats," he explained to a conference of Cuban trade union leaders in January 1987. "It is time for every worker to know about the problems of his factory," he said. "You are the party's most important force in the battle to rectify errors, struggle against negative tendencies and build socialism and communism in our country." But this does not mean that workers should join with administrators in seeking to maximize the "profitability"—and accompanying bonuses—of a particular enterprise at the expense of other groups of workers or of society as a whole. In the transition to socialism, Castro explained to the trade union leaders, workers are not the collective owners of the factory or enterprise in which they happen to be employed. "The workers own all the factories in the country and it is in the interests of all workers to have all factories, schools, and services functioning well."[20]

While fully egalitarian conditions cannot be achieved short of communism, Castro explained at the January 1987 trade union conference, society will not march toward that historic goal unless conscious steps are taken to narrow inequalities in wages and living conditions. *Granma Weekly Review* reported that Castro "said that the wage reform [of the early 1980s] raised the salaries of those who were already earning a lot but forgot about the modest worker." If this were not corrected then "little by little we will fall into a society based on a hierarchy, with a series of social categories of all kinds and follow in the footsteps of capitalism in this respect."[21] To remedy this situation, the Cuban government at the beginning of rectification gave priority to raising the minimum wages and living conditions of the lowest-paid sections of working people, thus narrowing the gap between them and the highest paid.

At the same time, a new attitude toward work was fostered—something Guevara had placed great emphasis on in the opening years of the revolution, as Tablada recounts. As working people are drawn into the administration of the state and economy, they are increasingly attracted to work for the benefit of society, both nationally and internationally, not just for themselves and their families. At the November–December 1986 session of the party congress, Castro pointed to a delegate who had twice volunteered for internationalist missions in Angola, asking what material incentive could lead to such self-sacrificing conduct. "I wonder, what bonus could we give him, what mechanisms could we utilize with him and the many thousands of others like him?" Castro asked.[22]

In order to advance along this communist course, Cuban revolutionists placed at the center of the rectification process the revival of collective voluntary work on the most needed social projects. In his speech on the twentieth anniversary of Guevara's death, Castro explained that during the previous decade:

> Voluntary work, the brainchild of Che and one of the best things he left us during his stay in our country and his part in the revolution, was steadily on the decline. . . . The bureaucrat's view, the technocrat's view that voluntary work was neither basic nor essential gained more and more ground.

The political retreat inside Cuba during the latter half of the 1970s and early 1980s on fronts such as voluntary work, however, was mitigated by the internationalist response of Cubans to popular victories in Vietnam and Africa, and especially by the Nicaraguan and Grenadan revolutions in 1979. These victories inspired hundreds of thousands of Cubans to volunteer for internationalist duties in these countries and elsewhere. In response to escalating U.S. military pressure, millions of Cubans mobilized for the Marches of the Fighting People and joined in the newly established Territorial Troop Militia in 1980. "During this period," Castro explained at the Communist youth congress in April 1987, "I would say that the revolutionary spirit found shelter in defense activities, in the Territorial Troop Militia mobilizations, in military training, in the millions of hours dedicated to these activities."[23] The response of Cuba's working people to improve qualitatively the defense of the country and to aid those making revolutionary advances abroad held off some of the worst consequences of the retreat and reinforced values and attitudes of solidarity and self-sacrifice that could be called on with the opening of the rectification process.

Following 1986, voluntary social labor was revived on a level comparable only to the early years of the Cuban and Russian revolutions—but on a larger scale and with greater centrality to the revolution than even these earlier experiences. Tens of thousands of full-time volunteers joined "minibrigades" building day-care centers, housing, clinics, and other projects. Hundreds of thousands more Cubans volunteered after school or work and on weekends.

Castro called special attention to the grave consequences for Cuban women of the snail's pace in constructing new day-care centers prior to the relaunching of the minibrigade movement. Between 1980 and 1985, for example, only five new day-care centers in Havana had been planned, and only two had been built. Through the minibrigades, more than 110 were constructed in 1987–88 alone, making it possible for thousands more women to join the work force and participate more fully as equals. Castro told delegates to a November 1987 Havana provincial meeting of the Communist Party:

> Those who advocated reactionary ideas within the revolution argued that building a day-care center was a social expense. Social expenses were no good, investing in production was good; as if those who work in the factories were . . . male and female mules and not human beings, not men and

women with their problems, especially women with their problems. . . . And whenever they say no daycare center, you can be sure there is a technocratic, bureaucratic, reactionary concept at work.[24]

Most full-time minibrigade members were workers who volunteered to be released from their regular jobs for a couple of years, receiving whatever wage they had been getting in their workplace. The minibrigades took on the character of a growing social movement led by some of Cuba's most conscious and disciplined working people who were convinced that the brigades opened the road toward returning to proletarian methods of meeting Cuba's social needs. Minibrigades had first been launched in Cuba at the opening of the 1970s. Like voluntary work efforts in general, these projects were abandoned by the end of that decade as inconsistent with the new planning and management methods modeled on those in the USSR.

"The minibrigades, which were destroyed for the sake of such mechanisms," Castro said in the speech that serves as the prologue to this book, "are now rising again from their ashes like a phoenix and demonstrating the significance of that mass movement, the significance of that revolutionary path of solving the problems that the theoreticians, technocrats, those who do not believe in man, and those who believe in two-bit capitalism had stopped and dismantled."

◆

In the summer of 1989, three years into the rectification process, the growing political consciousness and self-confidence of Cuban working people collided with the corruption and privileges of a social layer in the state apparatus. In July 1989 Diocles Torralbas, minister of transportation and a member of the party's Central Committee, was convicted on corruption charges and sentenced to twenty years in prison. That same month Arnaldo Ochoa—a popular division general who had been awarded the medal of Hero of the Republic of Cuba in 1984 for his role in commanding troops in Ethiopia and Angola, and a longtime Central Committee member—was convicted on charges of drug trafficking and treason and executed, along with two high-ranking officials in the Ministry of the Interior and another army officer. In August, José Abrantes, the minister of the interior and a Central Committee member, was convicted of misuse of government funds and abuse of authority and sentenced to twenty years.

In his speech before Cuba's Council of State reviewing the conviction and sentencing of Ochoa, Fidel Castro pointed to the "two worlds" in Cuban society whose conflict had been brought into the open by such cases of high-level abuse and corruption. "What do the lives of these gentlemen have to do with the life of a worker?" Castro asked. "What do the customs of these gentlemen have in common with the customs of our working class? They are two different worlds. And we cannot rest until there is one single world here: not the world of the bourgeoisie or the petty bourgeoisie, but the world of our workers, our working class, our proletariat, our farmers."[25] Castro's speech, and the remarks of all the other members of the Council of State, were broadcast nationwide on Cuban television. It was notable that several members of the body emphasized the necessity of returning to the course charted by

Che Guevara if the social chasm revealed by the Ochoa affair was to be closed.

The wherewithal to continue the volunteer construction brigades and social advances that marked the opening years of rectification, however, evaporated at the opening of the 1990s as a result of the severe economic shortages and dislocations caused by the collapse of Cuba's trade with the countries of Eastern Europe and the Soviet Union; this trade had previously accounted for some 85 percent of Cuba's imports. Imports from Eastern Europe virtually disappeared by the end of 1990; in 1991 imports from the Soviet Union plummeted to only 30 percent of their 1989 level and have plunged further since then. Overall, Cuba's imports were reduced by almost 60 percent over that two-year period. There are acute shortfalls of oil, grain, animal fodder, basic foodstuffs, construction materials, spare parts, and other goods. Reserves of foreign currency are under enormous strains.

As a result of this rapid and drastic contraction in imports, and consequently production, the Cuban government and Communist Party have initiated a package of measures aimed at meeting the requirements of what they call a "special period in peacetime." Not only has construction been stopped on social projects, but strict priorities have had to be placed on capital investments, allotments for major civil engineering projects, and purchases of raw materials and spare parts and renewal of amortization funds for many state enterprises. Resources and labor have been channeled toward projects deemed most essential to advancing self-sufficiency in food production and increasing hard currency earnings to purchase vital energy and industrial imports.

In his opening speech to the Fourth Congress of the Communist Party in October 1991, Castro summarized some of the consequences of the collapse in Cuba's trading links:

> Many people still don't understand what the special period is and the problems it entails. Many are still dreaming about things that we were doing, problems we were solving, and which we had to suspend suddenly when starting with the process of rectification we carried out a large-scale program in a series of fields. We were building housing at a tremendous rate; we had reorganized the minibrigade movement, for example. We were giving an enormous boost to the production of building materials. . . . There was cement for all of the social projects, housing, economic projects, hotels and everything else.
>
> That is, starting with the process of rectification, we tackled many problems in order to solve many of the material difficulties we had. . . . We didn't lose a minute, but used the few resources we had to boost all of those plans. We built child-care centers, special schools, polyclinics, and hospitals.[26]

What the Cuban revolution has accomplished since 1990 in the face of such unprecedented economic blows is something no capitalist country in the world could have done. In fact, it is something that Cuba itself could not have done had working people not gained confidence through the rectification process by taking on bureaucratic resistance to their collective efforts to keep the revolution moving forward. The revolution's capacity to survive is a product of the political consciousness and spirit of volunteer labor on the part of millions of Cuban toilers.

In face of acute shortages of fuel and other inputs, the Cuban government mobilized large numbers of volunteer cane cutters to minimize the depletion of scarce petroleum resources in tractors and mechanized harvesters; the sugar harvest dropped in 1991 and fell even further in 1992. Workers and farmers on state farms and cooperatives are using growing numbers of oxen in farm production and transport during the "special period." Large quantities of bicycles have been imported, and begun to be produced in Cuba, to compensate for necessary cuts in the extent and frequency of public transportation. Private energy use and purchase of gasoline have been sharply curtailed. Shortages of energy, raw materials, and spare parts have led to the shutdown of factories and a shortening of working hours and days in other enterprises.

The government has taken steps to ensure that the greatly reduced quantities of necessities (either imports or items dependent on imports for their production) are distributed as equitably as possible. Virtually all food items (except fresh fruits and vegetables), clothes, soap, and other basic consumer goods in very short supply are strictly rationed. While the shortages bring substantial hardships, and the distribution system is plagued with bureaucratic inefficiencies, the assurance through the rationing system that everyone gets an equitable, even if small, amount of what is available is welcomed by most working people in Cuba.

The construction of new housing, child-care centers, and other social projects has been halted, and the special contingents pared back. The momentum from the volunteer labor mobilizations during the opening years of rectification, however, has been redirected toward a major effort to achieve food self-sufficiency in Cuba. Hundreds of thousands of Cubans have volunteered for intensive two-week work brigades in the fields of state farms. Special contingents of volunteers who sign up for a couple of years are constructing dams and expanded irrigation systems and waterworks, as well as providing a skilled work force in agriculture. In Havana and other cities, a major focus of construction is on refrigerated storage depots for farm produce and an expanded network of distribution centers. As a result, there has been a marked increase in the availability of vegetables, tubers, and fruits since the food program began. There is growing confidence among working people that Cuba will, over time, be able to meet its food needs.

Dependency on food imports in Cuba—as throughout the countries of Latin America and the Caribbean, Africa, and most of Asia and the Pacific—is a legacy of imperialist superexploitation. Cultivation and animal husbandry to feed the population in these countries were destroyed and arable land used to raise export crops to profit imperialist businesses, while meat, grain, and processed foods were imported from Europe, North America, Japan, Australia, and New Zealand. In the "underdeveloped world, in the world of hunger," Guevara told an international trade conference in March 1964, "projects for increasing food production— that is, to be able to eat—are actually discouraged in order to maintain present prices. This is the inexorable law of the philosophy of plunder, which must cease to be the rule in relations between peoples."[27]

"In terms of agriculture," Guevara said in a 1961 speech, "Cuba has set itself the goal of reaching self-sufficiency in the production of food," centering on crops and meat products suited to its soil and climatic conditions.[28]

This goal, too, was a victim of the turn toward the economic planning priorities of the Soviet Union and Eastern Europe in the early 1970s, which accompanied Cuba's entry into the Moscow-dominated trading bloc, the Council for Mutual Economic Assistance (CMEA). Cuba's initial steps toward food self-sufficiency were largely shelved, as the role assigned to Cuba in what the CMEA considered an "international socialist division of labor" was the export of sugar, citrus fruit, and nickel and the import of many food products along with light and heavy industrial goods. Steps initiated during rectification to begin redressing this imbalance were necessarily accelerated in the early 1990s, when both the CMEA and Cuba's long-standing trading patterns simultaneously disappeared.

With the aim of rapidly increasing hard currency earnings, the Cuban government is giving priority to investment in tourism, nickel production, and medical and pharmaceutical products. It is encouraging joint ventures with foreign capital to expand investment in these sectors and pry open markets to counter the pressures of Washington's embargo.

The difficult conditions during the "special period" provide a new rationalization for privileged layers within the state and party apparatus to argue that whatever the merits of Guevara's economic and social perspectives on the transition to socialism, now is not the time to begin applying them in Cuba. The opposite is the truth, however.

In the speech that opens this book, Fidel Castro insists that the views fought for by Che in the opening years of the Cuban revolution are "absolutely relevant today, ideas without which I am convinced communism cannot be built."

That remains the challenge to working people and revolutionaries in Cuba today. Given their determination to surmount the enormous difficulties created by the economic and political pressures of U.S. imperialism, compounded by the collapse of economic relations with the former Soviet Union and Eastern Europe, now more than ever the challenge is to move toward reorganizing economic planning and management, and the social relations that underlie them, along the lines championed by Ernesto Che Guevara that are described in the pages that follow.

As this book amply demonstrates, Guevara's perspectives—codified in the budgetary finance system—were not disconnected proposals, practical only in "the best of times." They were an integrated approach to organize and mobilize the collective labor of working people to adjust to whatever particular objective conditions they confronted. They provided a framework for the working class, in alliance with toiling farmers, to structure the economic and social organization of its state and economy to advance the construction of socialism, and in the process to transform themselves into a more politically conscious, self-confident, and proletarian component of an internationalist communist movement.

Carlos Tablada, born in 1948, is an economist who teaches at the University of Havana and has worked in the management of Cuban state enterprises. He is an associate of Cuba's Center for the Study of the Americas and of the Center for Research on the World Economy. His manuscript of this book, completed in 1984, was awarded the Ernesto Che Guevara Special Prize in the 1987 literary competition of the Havana-based cultural institution Casa de las Américas.

A first edition of Tablada's manuscript was published in Cuba in 1987 in two limited printings with the title *El pensamiento económico de Ernesto Che Guevara* (The economic thought of Ernesto Che Guevara). When a second edition was published under the same title by the publishing house of Casa de las Américas in early 1988, it became a best-selling title. The initial run of 250,000 was sold out in Cuba within weeks.

This French edition has been translated from the manuscript of a third Cuban edition, and incorporates several additional citations from Guevara's works suggested by the author. The translation into French was done by Leonor Goldstein Mayero with the help of a team of volunteers in Paris and Montreal. The French edition was edited by Michel Dugré of Montreal.

Since the publication of this book in Spanish, Tablada has traveled widely, speaking on Che Guevara's political and theoretical contributions and their relevance to the Cuban revolution today. In Latin America he has visited Argentina, Bolivia, Chile, Ecuador, Mexico, Nicaragua, Panama, Peru, and Venezuela, more than once in several cases. In the fall of 1989 he conducted a two-week speaking tour of Canada. In April–May 1990 he spoke in some thirty cities and towns across the United States, returning in November–December 1991 for another U.S. tour of fifteen cities. In late 1990 and early 1991, Tablada toured ten countries in Western Europe: Britain, Denmark, the Faeroe Islands, Finland, France, Greece, Iceland, Norway, Spain, and Sweden. He has spoken in Italy in 1988 and 1989. The publication of this French-language edition coincides with a fall 1992 European speaking tour.

Footnotes to the quotations used in the text indicate a French-language source when one exists. However, we have translated from Spanish all quotations from Guevara with the exception of those from "Socialism and Man in Cuba," which we have taken from the pamphlet of the same name published in French by Pathfinder in 1989. The list of further readings indicates the works of Guevara that have been published in French. Translations of quotations from V.I. Lenin that appear in the text are taken from the French-language edition of Lenin's *Collected Works* (Moscow: Progress Publishers). Minor editorial improvements in these translations have been made in a few cases.

The most complete edition of Guevara's writings and speeches in print is the nine-volume *Ernesto Che Guevara: Escritos y discursos* (Havana: Editorial de Ciencias Sociales, 1977). A seven-volume edition of Guevara's works published in limited numbers by the Ministry of Sugar in 1967 has long been unavailable. The extensive bibliography compiled by Tablada and published here lists the contents of most of the Ministry of Sugar edition and indicates the breadth of Guevara's writings and speeches. Much work still remains to bring this material as well as many unpublished manuscripts and speeches by Guevara into print. We hope that Pathfinder's publication, first in English and now French, of this survey of Guevara's contributions is a step toward the publication of more and more of his works and their translation into both languages in coming years.

We are grateful for the photographs that have been made available for this edition by Prensa Latina and *Granma* newspaper.

AUGUST I, 1992

NOTES

1. Fidel Castro, speech closing City of Havana provincial party meeting, November 29, 1987, in *Militant*, January 29, 1988. Also found in *Granma Weekly Review* (hereafter *GWR*), December 13, 1987.

2. Castro's October 8, 1987, speech commemorating the twentieth anniversary of Guevara's death, is contained in *Che Guevara: Economics and Politics in the Transition to Socialism* (New York: Pathfinder, 1989) under the title "Che's Ideas Are Absolutely Relevant Today."

3. Che Guevara, "The Real Meaning of the Alliance for Progress," August 8, 1961, in *Che Guevara and the Cuban Revolution* (New York: Pathfinder, 1987), p. 276.

4. Guevara, *Socialism and Man in Cuba* (New York: Pathfinder, 1968, 2009), p. 13 [2017 printing].

5. Castro, "Important Problems for the Whole of Revolutionary Thought," December 2, 1986, in *New International*, no. 6, 1987, p. 352 [2014 printing]. Hereafter *NI*. Also found in *GWR*, December 14, 1986.

6. Articles by Guevara from this debate in the early 1960s, together with discussions from the late 1980s and early 1990s of Che's views, appear in issue no. 8 of the English-language magazine *New International* and in issue no. 2 of its Spanish-language sister publication *Nueva Internacional*. The issue is entitled "Che Guevara, Cuba, and the Road to Socialism."

7. Castro, "Che's Enduring Contributions to Revolutionary

Thought," October 18, 1967, in *Che Guevara and the Cuban Revolution*, p. 26.

8. Nelson Mandela, speech in Havana, July 26, 1991, in Mandela, Castro, *How Far We Slaves Have Come!* (New York: Pathfinder, 1991), p. 20 [2017 printing].

9. Mandela, *How Far We Slaves Have Come!*, p. 22.

10. Castro, "Important Problems," in *NI*, no. 6, 1987, p. 352.

11. Castro, "Important Problems," in *NI*, no. 6, 1987, p. 351.

12. Castro, "Renewal or Death," February 7, 1986, in *NI*, no. 6, 1987, pp. 390–91.

13. Castro, speech at closing session of the Fifth Congress of the Union of Young Communists, April 5, 1987, in *Militant*, May 29, 1987. Also found in *GWR*, April 19, 1987.

14. Castro, "Important Problems," in *NI*, no. 6, 1987, pp. 356–57.

15. Castro, speech of July 26, 1988, in *Cuba Will Never Adopt Capitalist Methods*, (New York: Pathfinder, 1988), p. 26 [2014 printing].

16. Castro, "Important Problems," in *NI*, no. 6, 1987, pp. 357, 368.

17. Castro, "Important Problems," in *NI*, no. 6, 1987, p. 358.

18. Castro, speech to Union of Young Communists, in *Militant*, May 29, 1987.

19. Castro, "Important Problems," in *NI*, no. 6, 1987, p. 361.

20. Castro, speech to plenary meeting of the National Council of the Central Organization of Cuban Trade Unions, January 14, 1987, in *GWR*, February 1, 1987.

21. Castro, *GWR*, February 1, 1987.

22. Castro, "Important Problems," in *NI*, no. 6, 1987, p. 368.

23. Castro, speech to Union of Young Communists, in *Militant*, May 29, 1987.

24. Castro, speech closing City of Havana provincial party meeting, November 29, 1987, in *GWR*, December 13, 1987. Also found in *GWR*, July 23, 1989.

25. Castro, speech to Council of State, July 9, 1989, in *Militant*, August 11, 1989.

26. Castro, opening speech to Fourth Congress of Communist Party of Cuba, October 10, 1991, in *Granma International*, November 3, 1991.

27. Guevara, "The Philosophy of Plunder Must Cease," March 25, 1964, in *Che Guevara and the Cuban Revolution*, p. 313.

28. Guevara, "The Real Meaning of the Alliance for Progress," August 8, 1961, in *Che Guevara and the Cuban Revolution*, p. 288.

BY MARY-ALICE WATERS

In Defense of the US Working Class

Drawing on the fighting traditions of the oppressed and exploited of all colors and national origins, in 2018 tens of thousands of teachers and other working people in West Virginia, Oklahoma, and other states waged victorious strikes. They fought for dignity and respect for themselves, their families, and for all working people. $7. Also in Spanish, French, Farsi, Greek.

Is Socialist Revolution in the US Possible?
A Necessary Debate among Working People

Fighting for a society only working people can create, it is our own capacities we will discover. And we will answer the question posed here with a resounding "Yes." Revolution is possible but not inevitable. That depends on us. $7. Also in Spanish, French, Farsi.

Che Guevara, Cuba, and the Road to Socialism
ERNESTO CHE GUEVARA
CARLOS RAFAEL RODRÍGUEZ
CARLOS TABLADA, MARY-ALICE WATERS
STEVE CLARK, JACK BARNES

Exchanges from the opening years of the Cuban Revolution and today on the political perspectives defended by Guevara as he helped lead working people to advance the transformation of economic and social relations in Cuba. In *New International* no. 8. $14. Also in Spanish.

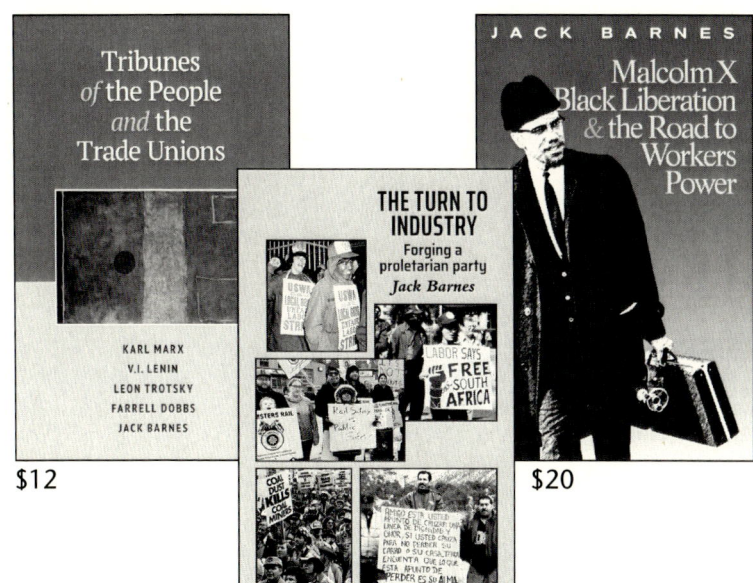

$12

$20

$15

Three books to be read as one...

about building a party that's working class in program, composition, and action. One that recognizes, in word and deed, the most revolutionary fact of our time...

... that working people have the power to create a different world as we act together to defend our own class interests—not those of the privileged classes who exploit our labor, not of those who fear us as "deplorables," or just plain "trash."

As we advance along a revolutionary course toward workers power, we will transform ourselves and awaken to our own worth. Also in Spanish, French, Farsi, Greek.

Special Offer!
All three $30

The Turn to Industry and *Tribunes of the People and the Trade Unions* $20

Either book plus *Malcolm X, Black Liberation, and the Road to Workers Power* $25

PATHFINDERPRESS.COM

WORKING-CLASS LEADERSHIP AND THE SOCIALIST REVOLUTION

New Edition!
Che Guevara on Economics and Politics in the Transition to Socialism
CARLOS TABLADA

It's essential for working people to win state power, said Ernesto Che Guevara. "Then there's the second stage, maybe more difficult than the first"—the transition from dog-eat-dog capitalism to socialism. That includes moving from work as a condition for survival, to voluntary social labor through which we express our common humanity. Includes Fidel Castro's 1987 speech "Che's Ideas Are Absolutely Relevant Today." New edition with substantially expanded selections from Guevara's writings. $17. Also in Spanish.

Lenin's Final Fight
Speeches and Writings, 1922–23
V.I. LENIN

In 1922 and 1923, V.I. Lenin, central leader of the world's first socialist revolution, waged what was to be his last political battle—one that was lost after his death. At stake was whether that revolutionary government and the world communist movement it led would remain on the revolutionary proletarian course that brought workers and peasants to power in October 1917. $17. Also in Spanish, Farsi, Greek.

Are They Rich Because They're Smart?
Class, Privilege, and Learning Under Capitalism
JACK BARNES

Exposes growing class inequalities in the US and the self-serving rationalizations of well-paid professionals who think their "brilliance" equips them to "regulate" working people, who don't know what's in our own best interest. $10. Also in Spanish, French, Farsi, Arabic, Greek.

BUILDING A PROLETARIAN PARTY

New!
The Fight Against Jew-Hatred and Pogroms in the Imperialist Epoch
Stakes for the International Working Class

V.I. LENIN, LEON TROTSKY
FARRELL DOBBS, JAMES P. CANNON
JACK BARNES, DAVE PRINCE

Jew-hatred and pogroms—such as Hamas carried out on October 7, 2023—are now part of the permanent social convulsions and wars of the imperialist epoch. The authors explain why fighting Jew-hatred is of decisive importance to the working class and oppressed nations of the world, and answer the question: *What is to be done to end it*—for all time. $10. Also in Spanish and French.

The Low Point of Labor Resistance Is Behind Us
The Socialist Workers Party Looks Forward

JACK BARNES, MARY-ALICE WATERS, STEVE CLARK

The global order imposed by Washington after its victory in World War II is shattering. A long retreat by the working class and unions has come to an end. The bosses and their government are stepping up attacks on our wages, conditions, and constitutional rights. This book highlights opportunities for building a mass proletarian party able to lead the struggle to end capitalist rule, opening a socialist future for humanity. $10. Also in Spanish, French, Greek.

Teamster Rebellion

FARRELL DOBBS

The 1934 strikes that won union recognition for truckers and warehouse workers in Minneapolis and helped pave the way for the working-class social movement that built the industrial unions. The first of four volumes by a central leader of these battles. $16. Also in Spanish, French, Farsi, Greek.

PATHFINDERPRESS.COM

EXPAND YOUR REVOLUTIONARY LIBRARY

Labor, Nature, and the Evolution of Humanity
The Long View of History

FREDERICK ENGELS, KARL MARX
GEORGE NOVACK
MARY-ALICE WATERS

Without understanding that social labor, transforming nature, has driven humanity's evolution for millions of years, working people are unable to see beyond the capitalist epoch of class exploitation that warps all human relations, ideas, and values. Only the revolutionary conquest of state power by the working class can open the door to a world free of capitalist exploitation, degradation of nature, subjugation of women, racism, and war. A world built on human solidarity. A socialist world. $12. Also in Spanish and French.

Thomas Sankara Speaks
The Burkina Faso Revolution, 1983–87

Under Sankara's guidance, Burkina Faso's revolutionary government led peasants, workers, women, and youth to expand literacy; to sink wells, plant trees, erect housing; to combat women's oppression; to carry out land reform; to join others worldwide to free themselves from the imperialist yoke. $20. Also in French.

Cuba and the Coming American Revolution
JACK BARNES

This is a book about the example set by the Cuban people that socialist revolution is not only necessary—it can be made. A book about the struggles of workers and other exploited producers in the imperialist heartland, and the youth attracted to them. About the class struggle in the US, where the revolutionary capacities of working people are as utterly discounted by the ruling powers as were those of the Cuban toilers. And just as wrongly. $10. Also in Spanish, French, Farsi.

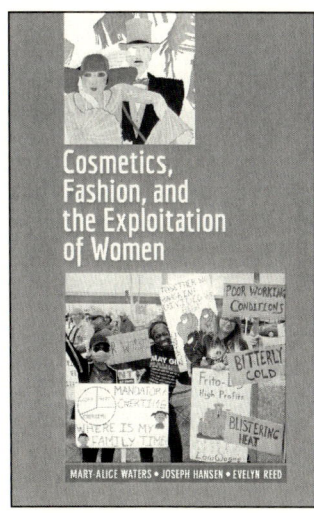

New Expanded Edition!
Cosmetics, Fashion, and the Exploitation of Women
MARY-ALICE WATERS
JOSEPH HANSEN, EVELYN REED

"Norms of beauty and fashion are inseparable from the class struggle" is the new opening chapter of this timely expanded edition of a lively 1950s debate in the *Militant,* a socialist newsweekly. How cosmetics and fashion monopolies rake in profits from social insecurities of women and adolescents. Why women's integration in the workforce and unions marks a major advance in the fight for their emancipation. A Marxist classic on the origins of women's oppression and the working-class road forward. $15. Also in Spanish, French, Farsi, Greek.

Malcolm X: The Last Speeches

"Any kind of movement for freedom of Black people based solely within the confines of America is absolutely doomed to fail." Speeches and interviews from the last two years of his life. $12

Pathfinder Press **accessible e-books** for the blind, those with low vision, or other challenges reading print books

For a list of current accessible titles, go to: pathfinderpress.com/collections/books-for-the-blind.

Visit bookshare.org for information on how to sign up.

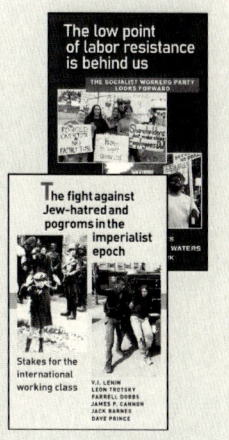

PATHFINDERPRESS.COM

PATHFINDER AROUND THE WORLD

UNITED STATES
(and Caribbean, Latin America, and East Asia)
> Pathfinder Books, 306 W. 37th St., 13th Floor
> New York, NY 10018

CANADA
> Pathfinder Books, 7107 St. Denis, Suite 204
> Montreal, QC H2S 2S5

UNITED KINGDOM
(and Europe, Africa, Middle East, and South Asia)
> Pathfinder Books, 5 Norman Rd.
> Seven Sisters, London N15 4ND

AUSTRALIA
(and New Zealand, Southeast Asia, and the Pacific)
> Pathfinder Books, Suite 2, First floor, 275 George St.
> Liverpool, Sydney, NSW 2170
> Postal address: P.O. Box 73, Campsie, NSW 2194

BUILD YOUR LIBRARY!
JOIN THE PATHFINDER READERS CLUB

$10 / YEAR
25% DISCOUNT ON ALL PATHFINDER TITLES
30% OFF BOOKS OF THE MONTH
Valid at pathfinderpress.com and local Pathfinder book centers

Go to: pathfinderpress.com/products/pathfinder-readers-club

Pathfinder
pathfinderpress.com